Wicca fo

A Guide to Real Wiccan Beliefs, Magic and Rituals

Table of Contents

Introduction

Chapter 1:What is Wicca?

Chapter 2:Rituals and Spells

Chapter 3:Mythology

Chapter 4:How to Get Started

Final Words

Introduction

This book contains proven steps and strategies on how to follow the path of Wicca.

The pentacle may be the symbol most associated with vicious, demonic forms of Satanism but this very same symbol is used in the modern day to represent one of the kindest, gentlest, and most endearing religions there have ever been. Wicca.

If you thought that Harry Potter was charming and helped in changing the attitudes of many who thought that sorcery and magic were nothing but trouble or silly little tricks, then Wicca will astound you just the same.

With charming mythology that chooses to try to explain, rather than to condemn; to empower, rather than deny; to show, rather than tell... it's a wonder why more peace-loving, calm spirits have not found their way to this old European religion.

Most religions have the best of intentions, but so many of the most popular religions happen also to be the most likely to inspire bigotry, violence, and countless evil acts in the name of righteousness. Wiccans and those like them have been condemned time and again for not fitting in with this holy pack, but perhaps it is for the better that they don't.

Wicca does not discriminate, it does not attack. Wicca does not command its practitioners to do anything but what they wish to do and it does not try to justify evil. And yet it has often got a bad rap. For being a stem-off of Satanism, for being a sex cult, for being just another new age pagan offshoot for the crazies and the misfits. But, these are just some of the lies you will see exposed.

And, if you already know the truth and are more than curious to get started on your own path to The Craft, you will be delighted by what you find within. You will learn about real witchcraft. It may not sparkle, but it certainly does work. You will understand the balance and harmony created through the God and Goddess of Wicca, and the symbolism that represents them. You will get to know the Wiccan holy days and why they are celebrated, and how. You will be given a step-by-step guide on how you can get started finding a coven, creating your own altar, and even your own book of shadows.

Along the way, you might even get a tad bit of a history lesson on Gerald Gardner, the founder of the original Wicca, and you might learn a thing or two you hadn't planned to while you're at it. The parallels drawn to other religions means you may learn more than a little bit about other belief systems while you're learning about the one in the title, and the mythologies and symbolism they come with.

If you're just a curious wanderer, then please come in. You are invited to understand. If everyone could properly understand the beliefs of others, and stand to tolerate them, perhaps the world would be a far better place. By reading this book you will be given the opportunity to get to know the charming beliefs of the Wiccans you share the world with, and by doing so you will better understand the world and your place within it.

Thanks again and I hope you enjoy it!

Chapter 1: What is Wicca?

For those reading who may have only heard of Wicca in passing, or in movies, or only from the churches of other religions, there is a great likelihood that you will be surprised and disappointed by the contents of this ebook. An ebook which seeks to explain the ways of Wicca and the techniques used by Wiccans in their practice. In order to do that effectively, it is important that we start with what Wicca is not.

Wicca and Paganism are not the same, and Witchcraft is something different altogether. While it is certainly true that Wicca is a form of Paganism, to say that they are the same would imply that there are no differences between them and that all Wiccans are Pagans and all Pagans are Wiccans. While the former is true, the latter is not. There are many forms of Paganism which are vastly different from Wicca and calling them the same would be like relating a Maple tree to an Oak tree. They are alike because they are both trees of a similar kind, but they are called by different names because they are different.

Witchcraft, on the other hand, which most people know of mostly from Halloween stories and the historical Witch Trials, is not a religion and most likely never was. While there are some who connect Wicca and Witchcraft in order to make Wicca seem more ancient than it is, historians can not agree with people of such positions. The evidence simply isn't there. So, while Witchcraft of some form may be ancient, likely one of the most ancient religions in history, Wicca is not. And whereas Witchcraft is popularized as being concerned only with casting spells, Wicca is about far more than just sorcery.

Wicca is also not Satanism, nor is it violent nor demonic. Primarily because of its connections with Witchcraft and the fact that the world's most prominent religions have somewhere within their religious texts condemnation of sorcery, Wicca has been thrown in with negative religions and cults. Which is certainly not the kind of company any true Wiccan would ever want to be in. Wicca is a peaceful, personal religion. One of the main guidelines of the religion is "If it harm none, do as you will." Which is a nice, concise version of the same kind of commandments and sentiments given to humanity by hundreds of other spiritual leaders. It is, essentially, the golden rule.

Wiccans, Christians, Jews, Muslims, Buddhists, Taoists, Hindus and many others all follow the same rule. "Do unto others as you would have them do unto you" and "If it harm none, do as you will" are just different ways of saying the same thing.

Now lets talk a moment about the common lumping together of Satanism with Wicca and Witchcraft. It's important first to be clear about what kind of Satanism we're talking about here, because there are different kinds.

There is a benign Satanism which was formed by man named Anton LaVey, which is all about setting your own path in life, not walking on the eggshells laid out by other judgmental religions, and living the life you want to live and not the life as you are told to live it through dogma. There is some mention of some form of black magic and spells, but keep in mind that this may be metaphorical or satirical in nature as most Levayan Satanists do not worship nor believe in Satan or deities of any kind. This kind of Satanism is organized through churches, harmful Satanism is not.

Harmful Satanism does not even really exist as an organized group, but within disturbed individuals and cults alike. These kinds of Satanists may partake in murder, sex orgies, drug binges, human/animal sacrifices and even cannibalism inspired by a legitimate attempt to worship the Satan of The Bible.

Wicca is not affiliated with either group, but certainly not the second one. For Wiccans, there is no Satan, no devil of any kind, nor even a hell for that demonic creature to reside in. Harmful Satanism certainly does not follow the golden rule of "If it harm none, do as you will" and that means it has no right being lumped together with Wicca.

Wicca is not a sex cult. Let it be known that Wicca is a religion with a prominent respect and pedestal reserved for the sexual, but that is not to say that sex is all Wicca is about. As we will delve in more deeply later, Wicca is a lot different than the more popular Abrahamic religions (Christianity, Judaism, Islam) in that it does not shun the sexual and it does not exclude a matriarchal figure from the cosmos. In Wicca, there is both a God/Lord and a Goddess/Lady. Both a masculine and a feminine which work with balance throughout the Universe. Balance being the key word, not competition.

Sex is the single-most symbolic act of this harmony between the masculine and feminine powers and that is why it takes on an important role. The Great Rite is a ritual that celebrates the meeting of these powers. This can be displayed and felt through the symbolism of inserting a knife into a chalice, though it can also be achieved through actual sexual intercourse between man and woman (though homosexuality is not shunned by Wicca). Solitary practitioners, which is to say Wiccans that do not belong to a group or coven, can celebrate this harmony through masturbation.

It is important here to realize that the sexual nature of these rituals does not arise out of some perverse expression of lust. Lust is only ever that powerful when it is forbidden, and it is not forbidden in Wicca. While the Abrahamic religions do whatever they can to avoid the topic – praising virginity in women to a great extent, shunning sexual pleasures, excluding a feminine figure to balance the masculine, and even insisting that immaculate conception is the purest form because it does not involve any sexual relations... Wicca celebrates the sexual for its ability to bring about harmonious pleasure, unite the opposite powers, and bring new life into existence.

Being Wiccan in no way requires you to have sex with strangers, especially if you are underage. Sex is simply a way to celebrate what Wicca as a religion honors, it is not the only way.

So, then, what *is* Wicca?

Wicca is a religion, and not a practice, which was formed initially by Gerald Gardner in the early 1940's. He was inspired by the practices and beliefs expressed in the work of Margaret Murray on old witch cults, and went on to form the earliest iteration of the religion known as Gardnerian Wicca.

The specification of Gardnerian Wicca being the first iteration is to convey the message that, like many other religions, Wicca has branched off into several different groups. Each with their own views and practices which separate them from the initial tree. Also similar to many other religions, Wicca is a personal system of belief. That is to say that a group of Wiccans may believe in many of the same things, they may even belong to the same coven, but they will each give you noticeably different views on Wicca as a whole.

Unlike other religions, however, Wicca tends not to chastise nor talk ill of the belief systems or followers of other religions. This is because Wicca is a religion of harmony and balance. The Abrahamic religions (Christianity, Judaism, Islam) operate in accordance with old Zoroastrian views. Those being that there is a battle constantly raging throughout the world and universe between good and evil, between light and dark. They believe that, in the end, either the dark or the light must conquer the other. This leads to followers of these religions setting up heavy barriers between themselves and what they believe to be evil, what they believe to represent or be full of the darkness. They shun those outside the perimeters their religions set up for them to live within.

Wicca does not operate this way, because light conquering dark means that the world is out of balance. Evil conquering good, means harmony has been upset. This is why a God *and* Goddess are celebrated. They believe that these figures, which would seem to be opposed, actually live in harmony with one another, each contributing what the other cannot and providing the essential ingredients for the universe to exist as it does. The God and Goddess do not battle for supremacy, there is no long-lasting struggle for the light to conquer the dark. Because it is the light that helps cast the shadow, and it is the dark which provides the background to give light its vibrancy.

Practitioners of Wicca attempt to attune themselves to the natural order of nature, the natural rhythm of the universe – so that they can tell balance from imbalance, and so that they can work within rather than against that natural order. And it is out of this trickery, which might seem to others as foolishness, that Wiccan Magick arises. And, when you have finished with this ebook, you will have the understanding and the tools required to begin

on this path to harmony. Keep reading, allow your mind to be still, and let yourself feel the words as you read them. You still have much to learn.

Chapter 2: Rituals and Spells

Wicca, despite not being restricted only to witchcraft, is still known for its ambitions to work within the natural order to create change, to improve life, and to impact the Universe through magic. Wiccan magick, however, is different to the kind of magic you have seen in movies and read about in books. Other than the addition of a 'k', the most notable difference is that the magic of real life, the kind of magic that practitioners of Wicca attempt to use, does not spark and flare, it does not explode nor does the tip of their wands or flesh of their palms sparkle with a bright white, orange, or yellow glow. Wiccan magick is not supernatural by any means, unlike the magic you have heard of. It is entirely natural. Part of the natural order of the universe. And, it operates at a level that is difficult to perceive at times, but which can be seen all around you when you are attuned to the order within the world. All that glitters is not gold, and Wiccan magick is barely perceptible except to those that know its ways.

Within this chapter, we will go over some of the more important rituals as well as some of the most useful spells within Wicca, but by no means will we be covering the entire spell book. In fact, no one could because new spells are being created every day. As we discussed before, Wicca is a very personalized religion. So is the process of casting spells. The exact wordage used in this chapter can be adopted, but the most powerful spells are those that are created by you, with your own words. Only you know what is most powerful to you and it is by harnessing your own inner power that the magick is able to work.

There are several important tools and certain knowledge that you will need to put the spells listed below to good use. do not worry, we'll cover it all in the last chapter. When you are finished with this book, you will know what you have to do to get started casting these spells and taking part in these rituals. At that point, you can glance back at this chapter time and again, when you need to, when you are ready.

Always remember, when casting spells, to follow the presiding rule of Wicca. "If it harm none, do as you will." The power of white magic is very great, if your intentions are honest and your needs are real. Black magic is not only a path of destruction towards others, but it is a path to your own destruction. Bit by bit, little by little, it can whittle away the true nature of your spirit. Use these spells and rituals wisely, and always give thanks for the power given and entrusted to you by the Lord and Lady. Blessed be.

Healing Spell

This spell can be used on anything and anyone, from infants to elders, from animals to your own body. Please remember that this spell is not to be used alone. Medical care is always recommended for serious injuries, this spell is to be used to assist the process not to replace it.

1. Relax with the injured person/creature nearby. Empty your mind – let your thoughts flow, do not try to stop them. But, let them pass by without judgment, without focusing on them. Allow this moment to be as it is, without trying to change it.

2. In your own words, invite the spirit guides to join you. Yours and the other persons/creatures. Everyone has a spirit guide, they are always there but you need to allow them to help by recognizing their presence.

3. You may feel them joining you, and you may not. But, they will be there regardless. Acknowledge them, thank them. Thank them for their kindness to you and to the person/creature in your presence. If they can, have the other person recall times where they felt their guide with them, helping them. Have them also express gratitude. Let any emotion arise and flow, do not inhibit. Let love and happy memories fill you. Try to stay in this state of mind, do your best not to worry. Slow your breathing, slow your mind.

4. Request that the spirits help you. Request that they help you, or the person/creature with you, recover and grow great and strong and healthy. Visualize it happening. Show the spirit guides with your imagination what you want. Show your burns disappearing, or the other person growing stronger as

the cancer leaves their body and their hair grows back, or the bird in your hand flying away as though their wing had never been broken. You understand. do not hope it will happen, *know* it will happen.

5. There is a place at your center, near your heart. It is the energy center of your being. Focus on it. Breath in, imagining your breath filling this space at your center. Imagine a light glowing and growing from within. See it as whatever color represents healing to you. Use your instincts. Is it green? Is it blue? Perhaps it is violet? There is no wrong answer, but it must feel right to you. Focus on the love and gratitude you have kindled, watch it amplify the light growing within.

6. Now, imagine this energy flowing out of you and into the injured. Your own hand, someone else's thigh, or paw. Imagine the glowing light creating a protective barrier around the injury. See the injury with your eyes, imagine the light with your mind. Breathe deeply and imagine the light growing stronger and warmer with each breath.

7. When you feel that you have done all you can and that the injury has been given all you have, let go. Clear your mind. Relax your body. Know that the injury has been given healing. Thank the spirit guides for their kind assistance and bid them an appreciative goodbye. From that point on, to empower the protection you only need to return to a place of calm and imagine the light growing from your heart center into the injury. To keep it strong, to help it heal.

Money Spell

Wiccan magick is meant to interact with the natural order, the catch? Everything's natural. Even money. We all need money – or, most of us anyway. Now, like the last spell, this spell isn't going to send a million dollar check straight to your mailbox for no reason. That would truly be supernatural. No. This spell is about attracting money to you through the natural order. Which means you may find dollar bills where before there were none, you may find greater success and promotions in your work where there was once no hope.

Here's how it works:

1. This is an imbuing spell, which means you will be imbuing your magick within an object and the object will help make you a magnet for money. The things you will need for this spell are a golden chain, a golden ring, and yellow candles. The gold need not be real gold – if you could afford real gold chains and rings, maybe you are not so much in need after all? So, as long as it is colored gold, it's fine.

2. Start by casting a circle of protection. Casting circles is some very essential magic, but it takes too much time to explain it here. Before you finish reading, you will know exactly what casting a circle is and how it is done.

3. Form a triangle with your yellow candles in front of you, then light each of them with focus. Place the gold chain and ring within the triangle before you.

4. Visualize the abundance you want to come to you, imagine it filling the triangle in front of you. Imagine this yellow light growing and building, imagine the money you need, the job you want, the car, the boat – whatever it is that you are seeking, imagine it filling the space between the triangle where the gold chain and ring are.

5. Chant the following:

Gold, gold, gold wealth I seek

all gold in the universe I just need a peek

Gold, gold, gold wealth I need,

for bills I must pay and friends I must feed

So may it be.

You can also use your own chant, but be sure it has power to you. Let it be something you can feel and relate to.

6. Run the gold chain through the gold ring, and wear it. Feel the wealth of the universe. Know that it is coming to you. Allow it to connect to you. Let the golden light fill you and resonate within. Wear the chain and ring together as often you can to bring wealth your way.

Love Spell

It has been said many times before, but there is no harm repeating – love is its own kind of magic. Familial love and romantic love, the love of a friendship, and the love of a pet. But, the most important kind of love is self-love. There are love spells out there waiting to find you, waiting to help you find the mate to your soul. But, that's not what will be provided here. Because, even if all the love spells in the world work their charm and lead your soul mate straight to your front door, there is no guarantee that your love will stay. There is no guarantee that the love you have attracted is the kind that you need. There is only one way to ensure either one, and that is to love thyself. To feel love from within, so that you do not need it externally. So that you do not require someone else's love to exist. Self-love is powerful magick and it will attract people to you in its own right.

So, below is a magick spell that will help you to love yourself. Even if you are unlovable.

1. Be seated somewhere peaceful. Somewhere that you feel truly alone with yourself. If it is by the brook, then go there. If it is in the woods, then go there. If it is in your room, or in the bathtub, go there and relax. Allow your mind to clear and let any stray thoughts to pass by.

2. Place your focus on your heart, your center. Just as you did with the healing spell. Imagine that you are breathing into this area and that with each breath in you are sucking in the love the universe has to give to you and that with every breath out your heart center and the loving energy within it are growing and glowing greater. Until it finds its way out of your body and spinning, twisting, shimmering all around you. Imagine all the things that you love without condition. Family members, friends, animals. Let the love flow, let it build and flow out from your heart center.

Read slow and with meaning the following:

The Universe spreads and the galaxies spin

and they do this with the power of love

Mother Earth grows even when it snows

and she does this because we are loved

She understands my wonder and even my sins

it's time I did too and felt power from within

The Lord and the Lady and everyone knows

that I am the embodiment of love

Give me guidance and grace

Show me the way

So mote it be

Once again, replace your own words for mine. This is an example. The words have greater power when they are your own and represent what you truly believe.

3. Let it all sink in. Listen to the words, know them to be true. If you feel resistance, let it go. Let the heart energy grow stronger, let your self-love expand until you know what you have said of yourself is true.

New Year Ritual

There is great power in the events that take place in our lives. Years are significant to us. As we age, we remember the years of first kisses and final goodbyes, births and deaths, celebrated victories and losses we struggled to embrace. But, the past is still the past. While some things are nice to hang onto, others drag us down – but they all keep us from moving forward with an open, energetic state of mind.

The New Year ritual is a way for Wiccans to leave the last year behind them and start again. Whether it was a good year or a bad year, it is a year that has gone by and cannot be changed. The only thing we can do is move forward and grow stronger, and that is what this ritual is all about. Letting us let go and move on.

1. It is always best to start spells and rituals with a clear, peaceful mind. Start by calming yourself and

allowing your thoughts to flow and let go of judgmental impressions. Go to your altar, if you have one (you will know how to create one by the end of this book), or a place where you will be able to relax uninterrupted.

2. Begin by recording what you seek in the new year. Be broad, and accepting. It is not important that you get the Lamborghini over the Ferrari, but rather that something of value be coming your way. If you want love, state it. If you want to grow stronger within, state that too. Write it down.

3. There are four elements, and you will interact with them one at a time. Starting with air. Light incense. There are many kinds to choose from, but sage or citronella are ideal for cleansing. And then state the truth for you and how you intend to leave the year behind. For example:

Lord and Lady

The year's come and gone

I am grateful for gifts received

I am ready to let go of misfortunes

The year to come is now waiting

Let it give greater gifts

And cure last year's maladies

I cleanse the past

Air as my ally

So be it

Breath in the incense, allow the negatives of the past leave you and allow the air to cleanse you entirely. It is normal to feel a certain emptiness at this point. Will yourself with the light. Bright, comforting light. And thank the God and Goddess for their generosity.

4. Light a black candle. The darkness of the wax sucks out the darkness within you and allows positivity to reign. Think of your misfortunes and troubles of the past year and release them into the flame. Let the fire disintegrate the past that was and let it fill you with a firey ambition for the year to come. Say:

Lord and Lady

The year's come and gone

I am grateful for gifts received

I am ready to let go of misfortunes

The year to come is now waiting

Let it give greater gifts

And cure last year's maladies

I set the future aflame with opportunity

Fire as my ally

So be it

And show gratitude to the God and Goddess.

5. Fill a chalice with water and sit with it in your hands. Allow your body to merge with the water, feeling the connection in your mind. Feel gratitude for the water you possess and its ability to purify your soul and your body. Let yourself become full with your gratefulness. And say:

Lord and Lady

The year's come and gone

I am grateful for gifts received

I am ready to let go of misfortunes

The year to come is now waiting

Let it give greater gifts

And cure last year's maladies

I purify my soul and forgive my mistakes

Water as my ally

So be it

And thank the God and Goddess.

6. Retrieve the paper on which you have written down your wishes for the coming year. Wrap it around a quartz crystal of any size. Then say:

Lord and Lady

The year's come and gone

I am grateful for gifts received

I am ready to let go of misfortunes

The year to come is now waiting

Let it give greater gifts

And cure last year's maladies

I ground my dreams to true life

Earth as my ally

So be it

Place the quartz crystal, covered in the paper, inside a small jar. Keep it safe. Keep it where you will remember it. Thank the God and Goddess. Thank each of the elements for helping to grant you your future. And let them go by patting the floor three times.

Make a Scrying Mirror

Divination is defined as the act of seeking to understand or know what will come in the future, or about subjects and topics which are unknown, through a supernatural means. Of course, for a Wiccan, there is nothing unnatural about tapping the future. Nothing is unnatural. It is all within the natural order, you just have to know how to make it work. And, that's exactly what we're going to go over here.

One of the most essential tools that any Wicca devotee could possess, if divination is their interest, would be a scrying mirror. This is a mirror which is consecrated through magic to offer psychic properties, boosting your ability to intuit the coming future. Here's how you make a scrying mirror:

1. Start with an object with a clearly reflective surface. The reason 'mirror' is used in the name is because the most reflective surface you could choose would be a mirror. Although dark obsidian is also great. If you choose a mirror, you will have to start by painting it a dark black.

2. Next you will need to make a mugwort infusion. does not that sound wonderfully magical? Mugwort is an herb. To make the infusion, start by placing the herbs into a jar. Any size will do, but the time between prep and consecration will depend on the size. Next, bring water to boil. When it is steaming and bubbling and boiling, pour enough into the jar to cover the mugwort. Screw on the lid to the jar, extra tight. When the outside of the jar is lukewarm, rather than scalding, you are ready to strain the mixture. Place your chalice under the strainer and allow the infusion to fill it with the herbs left behind.

3. Relax yourself and cast your circle. Call upon the God and Goddess to join you. Clear your mind, and then let the mugwort infusion spill over the mirror. Imagine the mirror awakening, growing in its vision.

Imagine that the mixture is enabling you greater sight. Sight that can see forward in time.

4. Chant nine times:

Show me what I wish to see

One glance I might sneak

Here I am sitting, watching

The future's what I seek

I ask you for the honor

You will show me what lies ahead

the story yet to be told

Dividing rich men from the beggars

and watching young souls grow to old

Let it be done

And then watch carefully for what the Lord and Lady show you within the scrying mirror. Thank them for their generosity.

Ostara Ritual

As you will learn in the next chapter, the Goddess of Wicca takes on a variety of roles throughout the year. But, it is in spring and summer that life comes back to the Earth and the life giver returns to her old ways. Wiccans celebrate this time of growth and new beginnings. Oftentimes these celebrations are experienced en mass with entire covens gathering together for ritual.

But, not all Wiccans belong to covens. There are lone Wicca followers out there, in fact there are many. However, they need not worry about their inability to celebrate the coming of the life-giving seasons. Because there is a simple, lovely ritual that they can take part in that is no less a celebration and no less a wonderfully spiritual event regardless of their lone nature. Here's how:

1. Start by casting a circle. you will learn how to do this in the last chapter, so just keep this in mind for the moment.

2. Find something that grows out of soil. A potted plant is always nice. Place two candles down, one on either side of the plant. These candles represent the God and Goddess and the plant represents the new life they are providing to the Earth.

3. Light the candles, and, while doing, chant the following:

Caring Maiden and Loving Mother

And Oak King Father above

Your presence has unfolded once more

Blessing me and the people I love

The sun shines brightly

The air is quite warm

We creep out of our homes to see one another

and celebrate your coming

and your loving

and care

May harmony reign

and happiness spread

Blessed be.

4. Envision the things you hope to achieve in the coming year. Imagine yourself succeeding, imagine the fruits of your efforts paying off and your rewards coming in one after another. Imagine your bounty, your harvest, your success.

5. Lastly, you may which to ask the Goddess Ostara to help you with your ventures. It is important that you ask her in your own words, and with meaning. do not

ask for anything you are not entirely sure that you want. Thank the Goddess. Close your circle.

Chapter 3: Mythology

Every religion comes with its own set of beliefs and mythological tales, Wicca is no different. What you are about to read explains the heart of Wiccan beliefs and the origin tales of those beliefs. In order to fully understand Wicca, and/or to fully commit to the religion, you must understand the foundations of what Wicca teaches its practitioners. Even if you are only a casual reader with no intention to actually become a Wiccan in your own right, the following information will prove invaluable to understanding and empathizing with friends and family that take part in The Craft.

Three-Fold Rule

One of the first and most essential presiding rules of Wicca is the three fold rule. It pairs together with the other presiding rule that was spoken of earlier, "If it harm none, do what you will". While other religions simply command you to observe particular rules and laws, Wicca explains their version of the golden rule by telling their practitioners that the universe works according to a three-fold rule. That rule being that what you put out into the world comes back around to you, but three times as strong.

There are many similarities with the common concept of karma. But, the major difference is that karma involves the concepts of past lives. Meaning that you could get good or bad karma depending on the things you did or ways you were in lives other than the one you are living. That is not the three-fold rule. The three-fold rule is far more cause and effect oriented. It's like how digging a hole to try trapping someone you dislike could come back around to bite you if you are tricked into falling in the hole instead. Except, with the three-fold rule this hole would be three times as deep and full of deadly creatures.

Basically, Wiccans believe that the universe works in accordance to a natural order and justice is a part of that order. If you are kind and nice and careful with the way you interact with the world and with others within it, then you have got nothing to worry about. In fact, there's something wonderful on its way to you as we speak. But, if you are not that kind of person and you have done a lot of wrong in your time, there are things three times as bad coming back to you. This does not mean you are doomed, however, but simply that you must learn and atone for your mistakes. Start doing good and living a positive lifestyle. Work off your punishments with good deeds and unconditional love.

You are not marred as imperfect or sinful or incomplete if you have done wrong or if you refuse to follow the Wiccan path. In Wicca, it is taught that we are all divine in our own ways. The only punishments that come upon us are the ones we initiate ourselves through our own negativity and the atrocities we commit. The rewards that we reap come to us in thanks for all the good we have done and all the positivity we have brought to the world. In Wicca, you are not born into anything and you do not inherit the wrongs of people before your time. Wiccan's, simply, believe the universe is just.

Horned God

As we established earlier, Wiccans are not monotheists. That is, they do not believe in a singular, lone God as Christians, Jews, and Muslims do. Instead, they believe in a balance of both God and Goddess figures.

Their God, sometimes called the "Horned God" because he is depicted with antlers or horns, takes on two individual roles. In some belief systems, these roles are actually two separate deities. Regardless, there are two masculine God figures. One is known as the Oak King and the other as the Holly King.

Oak King and Holly King

The legend is that the Oak King and the Holly King battle for supremacy, for the adoration and preference of the Goddess. If you find this difficult to understand if this battle is seen to actually take place between two aspects of the same God, just think about the goings on of your own mind. When your good conscience battles your temptations. When your better reasoning bows to your superstitions. When your anxieties get the better of your confidence. These are all just aspects of you, but they can fight each other and, sometimes, one of them wins.

In Wiccan belief, the Oak King gets the better of the fight at Midsummer or Litha (the name of a Sabbat – more on that in a moment), while the Holly King wins out in Midwinter or Yule. The Oak King reigns at his most powerful from Midsummer on until he loses in Midwinter to the Holly King, who then reigns the remainder of the time until Midsummer comes once again.

These battles and the supremacy won from them may be seen to help explain the nature of the weather and how it changes. Much like old Roman, Greek, and Nordic myths were known to do. Like in one particular myth which explained the lack of rainfall and the drying up of the crops by saying that Thor had lost his hammer. When the rain returned, it was because he had retrieved it again through a clever, and amusing ruse.

Like the mythology of the Horned God, and Thor, and the Gods and Goddesses of Rome and Greece, the Triple Goddess also has her own part in the story of life, according to Wicca.

Triple Goddess

The importance and graceful symbolism of the Wiccan Triple Goddess cannot be overestimated. In fact, there are branches of Wicca in which she is the only deity worshiped. But, regardless of if she gets all the honor and recognition to herself, or shares it with the Horned God, the Triple Goddess is composed of three parts. These parts do not fight each other as the two identities of the Horned God do. Instead, they are rather representative of the stages that the Triple Goddess goes through in a Wiccan calendar year (Oct 31 to Oct 30).

Maiden

The young girl, the virgin and as-of-yet innocent symbol of youth. The Maiden represents new beginnings, life changes, new ideas and identities. She represents the potential for what may come as separate for what has happened already. She represents the hope on the horizon.

Her time of power is in spring, where the deathly elements pervading the Earth retreat and the fallen rise again. When the plants and flowers begin to grow, the trees start to bud, and everyone embraces the elements once more. Now much freer to do so in the warmth and life-giving nature of spring.

The moon is very important when it comes to the Goddess, and each aspect of her is celebrated at different times of year. The Maiden is celebrated during the waxing moon. Which is the cycle from new moon to full moon. It is the ascent from darkness to light. Which fully symbolizes the nature of the Maiden, creating new opportunities and bringing about new hope where it had once vanished away.

Mother

At her core, the Goddess and her aspects really represent the life cycle of the female of the species. Once young and innocent and new to the world, and now grown wiser and stronger and able to bear new life to start the cycle again. The Mother is the second aspect of the Goddess, which represents fertility and the giving of life, fulfillment, and growth.

Summer is when the Mother is at her most powerful, and the early autumn as well. There is warmth and everything has come alive. The sun is mighty and warm, the moon is bright and illuminating. And no moon more than the full moon – which is when the Mother is most celebrated. As the full moon only truly lasts one single night, these celebrations are extra special for Wiccans and are celebrated thirteen times a year (more on this in a moment). Many consider the Mother to be the strongest aspect of the Goddess.

The full moon represents what the moon look like at its fullest, what the Goddess is at her peak of power, what a woman can be at her weak of strength. If there is anything that a mother would not do for their child, it is not known to mankind. There is not a job they will not do, a crime they will not commit, a sacrifice they will not make for the protection and proper rearing of their children. Even women who have been abused, and stifled, and victimized, who have been made weak, and cowardly, and feeble – even they can become courageous, and mighty, and ferociously powerful for the sake of their children. Many consider that a woman is at her peak when she has a family to fend for and take care of, and perhaps that is why the Mother aspect of the Goddess is represented by the full moon.

Crone

No life is complete without death. But, more importantly, without the descent away from the maximum. While in popular culture old age is sometimes viewed negatively and the old woman is a stereotype for lagging behind the times, this is not the view of the Wiccan Crone. The Crone is the final stage of the Goddess and while it is not as new and fresh as the Maiden, not as powerful and strong as the Mother, it is a wise and formidable spirit.

While, in some ways, she represents the time of dying and death, she represents the ultimate conclusion to life. Not the sad conclusion, not the unfortunate conclusion, but the graceful conclusion. In this stage, the Goddess Crone represents the winter – the season when so many things freeze up and die. But, as we established before, they do not die forever. The same trees whose leaves dry up and fall out will grow new buds that will grow once again. Without the Crone, the Maiden has no freshness. Without the Crone, the Mother has nothing to protect.

She is celebrated in the waning cycle of the moon, which is the descent from full moon back to darkness. It is this descent that initiates the new cycle and allows the moon to once again grow full in the night sky. What importance would the full moon have if it were there at all times? What hope would the waxing moon provide if there were no darkness in the end?

Esbats and Moon Cycles

Since we are on the topic of the moon, lets talk about the celebration of the moon cycles. As we've been talking about, depending on the stage of the moon, either the Maiden, Mother, or Crone aspect of the Goddess is celebrated by Wicca devotees. But, with the time of the Mother being so short and her celebration being the same way, the special full moon occurrences are marked down with a particular title. Esbat.

An Esbat is a celebration every time the moon is full. There are thirteen Esbats in a year. Most months have only one full moon. With there being four seasons to a year, each season can be roughly narrowed down to three months each. December, January, February for Winter (time of the Crone). March, April, May for Spring (early time of the Maiden). June, July, August for Summer (late time of Maiden, early time of Mother). And, September, October, November for Autumn (late time for Mother).

Since most months have only one full moon, there should be an average three full moons per season. But, sometimes there isn't. Sometimes there are four. These moons, the thirteenth full moon of the year, are referred to blue moons. Hence the term 'once in a blue moon', which is roughly once per year.

Sabbat Celebrations

There are eight Sabbats. These are celebrations of the changes of seasons for Wiccans. They come every year and you can celebrate them with or without a coven. Here are the times to celebrate:

Samhain – End of Summer

Imbolc – Sundown February 1st through the day February 2nd

Beltane – Either April 30th or May 1st

Lughnasadh – July 31st to August 1st

Yule – Winter Solstice in Northern Hemisphere, Summer Solstice in Southern Hemisphere

Ostara – March 21st

Litha – June 21st

Mabon – September 21st

There is much more detail that could be given as to how to celebrate these holidays, and much of it is out there to find. Some special celebrations are kept tight within Wiccan covens, but most are not. Search out what you can find and celebrate your own way! Remember that Wicca is a personal religion, do not let anyone tell you how you should honor the God and Goddess and the changing of the times.

Chapter 4: How to Get Started

Finding a Coven

Wiccan covens are guarded communities in some ways. It's not that they are afraid of new members, but you have to understand that many people are closer to their brothers and sisters of The Craft than they are their actual brothers and sisters. you have got to find the right place, the place you will fit it and feel at home. And sometimes that will not be easy. The question you have to ask yourself is – do I really want to be a part of a coven?

Because, if you do, you must accept that some covens are exclusive to certain genders while others are exclusive to people of certain social status (married, single, etc) and some are even exclusive to homosexuals. And, you know what? That's okay. It's their right to do that, they are forming their own tight-knit group. But, if you really want to be a part of a coven, you will have to search for the right one for you.

In some ways it is like trying to find a good dojo to learn from when you are trying to learn martial arts. Not all teaching styles, not all communities, and not all martial arts are going to fit. You have to be aware of your needs and wants. Once you do that, you will be way ahead.

But, if you make the decision not to find yourself a coven because you are independent or because finding one seems like too much hassle... that's fine. There are many lone Wiccans and they are no more and no less successful on their path than those that belong to covens.

What definitely will not change, however, whether you are a lone practitioner or part of a group, is your need for understanding the following information and having to put it into action for your path down the road of Wicca to be rewarding, and successful.

Creating an Altar

To list here the exact method of creating an altar would be offensive to the many different branches and multitudes of different kinds of beliefs within the Wiccan religion. What can be said is that the altar is meant to be something inviting, something that you feel a connection and closeness to. Not something intimidating or strange to you.

Much like finding a coven, finding an altar that puts you where you need to be to work your magick can be a struggle but it is absolutely rewarding. Some Wiccans are exceedingly specific with their altars, using special items to mark the East, North, West, and South – representatives of the four elements and so forth. Others are more personal in their approach, surrounding their altar with items that mean something to them personally. Anything from pictures of family and friends, to special gifts or family heirlooms.

Others believe that the need for an altar is obsolete, or completely optional. This is because some hold the belief that the external altar is only a formality, only a method. The real altar is within you. The real altar, which connects you and the divine, and is full of each element and even the fifth element of spirit, is within you.

Still, many people prefer to have their own personal altar because it helps them to focus and it brings them closer to their religion. In the same way that Christians will decorate their houses with crosses, or wear them, or how Buddhists will have statues of the laughing Buddha, Wiccans make their altars into shrines to their God and Goddess and to their dedication to their faith.

Casting a Circle

Tidy the area:

Start out by clearing the area physically. If you are inside, pick up the area and keep things placed neatly.

If you are outside, you may wish to brush away twigs and leaves and things out of your circle. Starting by physically clearing the circle helps you understand the bounds of the circle and the physical space you will be creating for yourself.

Meditate and determine the bounds of the circle:

At this point you have physically cleared the circle. Now you will want to spiritually clear it. Of old, scattered thoughts. Of negative, harmful energy that may be lingering. Relax your body and mind, imagine the bounds of the circle and imagine a protective barrier encompassing you within it. Just like you did for the healing spell earlier on.

Use real items to create the circle:

Some people like to go beyond using their minds to create the bounds of the circle. Some people will use rocks to create the outline of the circle, or they will literally mark the area. Depending on the ritual or spell you are preparing to take part in the procedure may differ. For instance, some Wiccans like to have four candles within their circle. One to represent the North (Earth), South (Fire), West (Water), and East (Air)

Bless the circle:

If you have chosen to use the candles, you could walk the boundary of the circle and light the candles one by one. You could also leave a trail of salt behind you, warding off unwanted visitors. You may also wish to invoke the spirits to help you bless the circle, or bless some water which you could then sprinkle around the circle while once again warding off anything that might drop by uninvited. And you will also want to define the purpose of the circle. What is the ritual you are preparing to do, and the spell? What are you seeking? State this and you give the circle its power.

Book of Shadows

The originator and founder of Wicca, Gerald Gardner, had his own one of these and so should you. A book of shadows is your own kind of sacred text. There is no presiding text to Wicca, like there is a Bible to Christianity, and a Koran to Islam. So, you are going to create your own.

You can start with a simple notebook or a three ring binder. You could even use a word processor, though many Wiccans believe a BOS (Book of Shadows) should be handwritten and consecrated just like your other religious tools.

Regardless, you will use your BOS to store everything you need,

Sabbat ritual instructions acquired by you online or given to you by your coven, along with dates.

Lists of herbs and their magical uses, or concoctions of many herbs put together.

Instructions for spells with your own added notes from things you have experienced or learned through experimentation.

The rules of your coven, if you belong to one – or the rules you set out to follow if you are lone.

There is so much that you can add to your book of shadows, but the important thing is that it is yours. You are to protect it with care and see it as just as sacred as your altar, and the circles you cast, and your relationship to nature as well as the God or Goddess of your focus. Create your own BOS and create your own destiny, create your own luck and future in life.

Final Words

You have learned about the nature of Wicca, and some of its history, but you have not learned it all. There is so much more to learn, and you cannot know the path you wish to follow unless you see where it came from. It is recommended that you look into the history of Wicca when you get the chance.

You have been teased with the promises of spells and the attractive lure of the magick rituals listed earlier. These are only some of the many still to discover, and still only a fraction of the many you will hopefully create on your own. Magick is within you, with effort and care you can find it and put it to the use it was always meant to play. It will work on you anyway – but, through Wicca you can know how and why.

You have been enlightened as to the mythology and reasoning behind the beliefs of Wicca. You have learned about the God's dual personalities and how they fight for supremacy, and the three stages of the Goddess and what each of her beautiful aspects represent and how they can be related to the cycles of a woman's life. And, how the seasons and the moon correspond.

Now you know what you have to go on to do, there are decisions to make and preferences to be acquired. Do you belong in a coven? And, if so, what kind of coven? What is it that you are seeking, and is it available to you? And, if you do not belong in a coven, how will you hold yourself to your dedications. How will you keep on the path you are starting down? Because living a magickal life sounds simple, and lovely, and charming in theory but it is harder when you must face the challenges of everyday living.

What will surround your altar, and why? What matters most to you? What gives you power? Knowing that will allow you to tap into that magick, that very personal magick, that is stuck inside of you. The kind that most of us never know. You can set it free and use it, but first you have to know how. And, the only the way you know how is by knowing what. What motivates you? What keeps you going?

You now know when to celebrate, whether it be the thirteen times a year that the moon is full in the sky or the eight times a year that changes are set into motion. To celebrate them properly, you will have much more to learn. But, it will be worth it. Because you will feel connected. A part of nature. A part of the changing, malleable turn of events throughout your life. You will be a part of the natural order, and through it you will be allowed to understand and to flourish.

Let the circles you cast protect you, and let your Book of Shadows grow to immense size. Let your spells function properly and your rituals lead you to the light of balance in your life. Blessed be.

57973732R00029

Made in the USA
Middletown, DE
18 December 2017